REGAINING MOTIVATION AT WORK

Simple steps to finding purpose and happiness in your work

Written by Caroline Cailteux

Translated by Jessica Foster

How do people adapt to organisational changes?

Should I think about changing career path to regain my motivation?

PUTTING MEANING BACK INTO YOUR WORK

- **Issue:** how do I identify sources of demotivation and take action to motivate myself?
- **Uses:** it is not always enough to be competent to work well, and fulfilment in our personal lives is not necessarily solid enough protection to help us cope with unhappiness in our professional lives. When we lack the strength to go to work and fulfil our professional goals, it is important to take the time to reflect on what can be implemented, before reaching breaking point.
- **Professional context:** human resource management.
- **FAQs:**
  - To regain motivation at work, should I focus solely on professional aspects?
  - How should I cope with professional stress that reduces my motivation?
  - How can I come up with solutions when faced with difficult situations?
  - Would I be more satisfied and motivated if I worked part time?
  - How do people adapt to organisational changes?
  - Should I think about changing career path to regain my motivation?

Although many companies call upon "motivated individuals" in their job descriptions, motivation is not a skill that some of us have and some of us don't. It is a dynamic, a certain chemistry between an individual and the context they are in. Motivation is something that is cultivated, and whatever your job, your colleagues, your manager and your company all have their roles to play so that you are happy there. Although it is not always possible for you to act on other people and change their behaviour, we hope that an analysis of your situation in the light of the following ideas will motivate you to get stuck in again rather than doing nothing and letting the situation fester.

MOTIVATION: THE BASICS

MOTIVATION, SATISFACTION OR COMMITMENT?

Motivation is often confused with ideas of satisfaction and commitment. In their work *Motiver, être motivé et réussir ensemble* ("Motivate, be motivated and succeed together"), Éric Cobut and Géraldine Bomal explain that satisfaction is usually about the impressions we have about our professional situation, whereas motivation is more to do with the driving force behind our behaviour. Satisfaction is a state of being (we are either satisfied or unsatisfied), whereas motivation is a dynamic, a process requiring effort to propel us in our professional context. When we are motivated, it is always in reference to something; there is no such thing as absolute motivation. These two authors distinguish the absence of motivation from 'demotivation'. There is in fact a subtle difference between not finding anything that makes you want to work hard and watching your desire to work hard disappear on account of the deterioration of your relationship to your working environment.

Commitment is another concept that can be confused with motivation. This concept mostly refers to the relationship the person has with the organisation and its members. Commitment corresponds to our degree of psychological identification with our work and influences our overall image. As various studies on commitment in organisations illustrate, including that of Howard Klein, Thomas Becker and John Meyer, there are different kinds of commitment:

- Commitment to work, which is linked to the space it takes up in our lives;
- Commitment to the organisation as a whole, which implies an alignment with its goals and values, a desire to make an effort for its benefit and a desire to remain part of it;
- Commitment to a career or profession;
- Commitment to a specific role ('job involvement').

Your job and professional relationship with the organisation thus influence the perception you have of your overall image as well as your motivation at work. If you are being negatively impacted by elements of your professional context, it is important to spend a moment reflecting in order to figure out where the shoe pinches.

EVOLUTION OF THE CONCEPT OF MOTIVATION

In her work on intuitive management, Meryem Le Saget informs us that there have been three generations of conceptions of motivation since the early 20th century.

"I get my tasks done"

The first generation is linked to the age of industrialisation, efficiency and productivity, offering a single interpretation for workers, with identical solutions for each of them. Here, being motivated means working out of fear of an employer, out of hope for obtaining better living conditions, or for earning enough money to feed a family.

"I contribute to the completion of work"

The second generation is aware of the concepts of satisfaction and dissatisfaction at work. The needs of employees are taken into account and are grouped into large hierarchical categories, as the satisfaction of the lower levels is necessary for access to the higher levels. This new generation understands that a motivated person, in order to stay motivated, needs to be listened to, needs a suitable position and needs their contributions to be recognised.

Maslow's hierarchy of needs

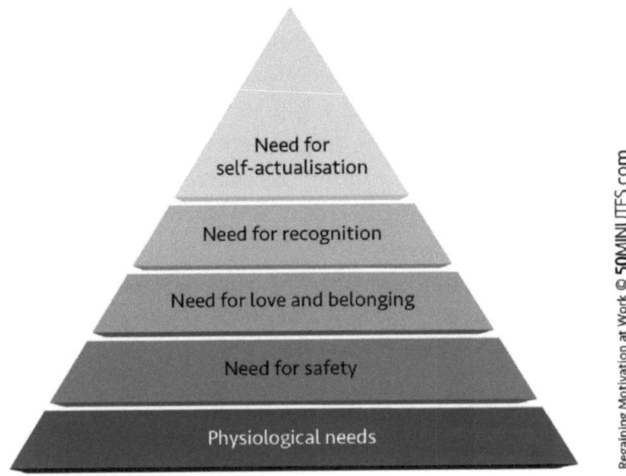

It was between 1950 and 1990, thanks to the human relations movement (a movement associated with the study of organisations following the Wall Street Crash of 1929, which studies group dynamics at work), that theories such as Maslow's started to promote the idea that not everyone has identical motivations.

Among other authors, the American psychologist Frederick Irving Herzberg (1923-2000) completes this approach with his two-factor theory, suggesting that we should pay attention to the balance between the presence and absence of factors of satisfaction and dissatisfaction. In fact, according to him, factors of satisfaction act independently of factors of dissatisfaction. Thus, if the absence of occupational hygiene factors (salary, good relationships, good working conditions, etc. – occupational hygiene actually concerns all the factors that affect the workers' health and wellbeing) leads to demotivation, the presence of motivating factors (return as a result of invested effort, nature of work, recognition, independence, etc.) will not necessarily prevent the worker from feeling dissatisfied in their work. This generation is about promoting the satisfying aspects while simultaneously working to reduce the factors of dissatisfaction. If an employer wants to motivate their staff, they must take their employees' needs into account, become aware of the factors of satisfaction and dissatisfaction and adapt solutions to the different scenarios.

"I commit to my work because I can express myself and be fulfilled"

Third-generation motivation appeared in the 1990s. Managers become leaders who are intuitive to systematic interpretations, and are committed to giving meaning back to work and treating people like adults. Beyond large categories, everyone is individual and solutions must therefore be tailored, but able to integrate into a complex system. It is no longer the task which is at the heart of motivation, but the interest in doing it.

Although the 1990s heralded the arrival of intuitive management, not all managers evolved at the same pace as the concept. It is not rare to observe managerial approaches that are centred on the division of tasks and the organisation of work, or based on participative management without having the slightest idea of what intuitive management might mean, the latter being based on the trust capital of their relationship with their employee and focused on the search for meaning in work.

GETTING 'RE-MOTIVATED': REFLECTION 1

Do I share my organisation's and/or my manager's conception of motivation?

If you feel unmotivated, it is possible that your idea of motivation and your expectations do not match those of your organisation or your manager. This is a first point of reflection which will allow you be aware of the reasons that might be behind your demotivation. Using the table below, which generation do your organisation and your manager most closely correspond to, in your opinion? And what is your own idea of motivation? Do you notice a mismatch?

FIRST GENERATION MOTIVATION	SECOND GENERATION MOTIVATION	THIRD GENERATION MOTIVATION
Management based on tasks and organisation of work. The carrot and stick approach is used.	Management based on types of needs, satisfaction and dissatisfaction.	Management based on intuition and the intrinsic motivations of intellectual curiosity, a wish to develop and a desire to make work meaningful.
My manager relies on technology and is only concerned with my efficiency, which brings me money.	My manager relies on his humanism and tries to understand how I work in order to maintain my enthusiasm and allow me to develop.	My manager relies on his intuition, trusts me and tries to make my work meaningful.

Contrary to what some people believe, the people around us cannot read our thoughts, cannot guess our expectations and do not necessarily conceive motivation in the same way; it is therefore important to express your opinions. Now that you have located the potential gap between your interpretation of motivation and that of your workplace, you need to articulate it. It goes without saying that the quality of the relationship and level of trust between you and your boss will make this step either easier or harder. However, the situation will not change if you keep this to yourself and never express it. Depending on your professional context, you will be able to address your message directly to your manager or potentially to a member of human resources, or to a member of support staff (appointed in the context of wellbeing at work) in order to look for constructive solutions.

To inspire you, here are some examples of feelings that you might want to articulate if your motivational expectations are at odds:

- "During our last meeting, we basically discussed the tasks I have to do. After that exchange, I felt a little disappointed, because I needed more feedback on the quality of my work. Could we set a time for a meeting to explore this in more detail, so that I can get a better sense of where I should be?"
- "During my evaluation meeting, we essentially talked about meeting objectives. When I left, I felt quite frustrated. I would like to have been given the chance to take a greater part in the project instead of having to make do with carrying out orders. Could we have a look at some of the strategic aspects of the projects together, so that I can be more independent in future?"
- "I appreciated the feedback you gave me last week. Despite all the positive points, I feel like I am losing energy. I need to make my job more meaningful. I have had a few ideas. Could we find a moment in the next few days to talk about the possibilities of developing my role within the team?"

WHAT IS THE PURPOSE OF MY WORK?

The tasks we have to do at work have a major influence on our motivation, satisfaction and productivity. Some researchers have therefore closely focused on what makes work meaningful, with 'meaningful' here denoting consistency between what an individual is looking for from their work and what they feel they are getting from the work they are doing. Eight main factors have been found to have an effect on whether or not employees find their work meaningful:

* respect for their values or work ethic
* autonomy
* the support they receive at work
* whether the work is useful
* opportunities for learning
* recognition
* quality of relationships at work
* the pleasure derived from finishing their work.

<u>**GETTING 'RE-MOTIVATED': REFLECTION 2**</u>

If you are feeling unmotivated, it might be because you no longer feel this consistency and your current job is no longer meaningful to you. You can then ask yourself the following questions:

* Do I feel that my values are being respected? Are we pursuing ethical principles, in my opinion?
* Do I feel that I can take initiative, offer solutions and organise myself freely?
* Do I feel that I am being supported, by my colleagues, superiors and organisation?
* Do I feel that my job is useful? In what ways is it useful? In what ways is it not useful, in my opinion?
* What were the last things I had the opportunity

to learn? When? Is that sufficient and satisfying?
- Do I feel that I am being recognised for my work? By whom? What kind of recognition do I need?
- Are my relationships at work pleasant, constructive and comfortable? Or rather, are they tense, unsatisfying and uncomfortable? With whom? Why is this?
- Generally speaking, what is it that I enjoy in a job?
  - Strong emotions, the chance to improve and exceed my expectations of myself.
  - The chance to learn or understand new things and satisfy my curiosity.
  - The chance to make what I do meaningful, to be fulfilled and to face challenges.

- Is this the case in the job I have currently?

For each answer to the above questions, ask yourself:

- What can I change directly?
- What can I change indirectly?
- What is it impossible to change?
- What solutions come to mind?
- What do I need to implement them?
- Who could I talk to about this?

THE DIFFERENT KINDS OF MOTIVATION

There are many different definitions of 'motivation'. Cassignol-Bertrand, François and Louche (cited in Gangloff: 2011), researchers at the Paul Valéry University of Montpellier and the University of Poitiers, inform us that the many authors who deal with the subject of motivation agree that it is a strength from inside or outside the self that triggers behaviour (with a certain intensity and in a certain direction) and ensures that it is sustainable. According to the theory of self-determination, our motivation can be considered as 'self-determined' when it relates to the actions that we choose and approve, and 'non-self-determined' when we impose things on ourselves or when they are imposed on us.

Intrinsic motivation

Intrinsic motivation comes from doing things that we want to do. It is highly self-determined and finds its origins in three different forms:

- Actions that give strong sensations, out of the desire to grow, to develop professionally and to show that we are capable of repeating an action indefinitely in order to improve;
- The pleasure of learning new things, finding out more about them, satisfying our curiosity or understanding things;
- The desire to make work meaningful, accomplishment, and the feeling of facing challenges.

Extrinsic motivation

Extrinsic motivation comes from doing things for instrumental reasons, 'in order to...'. It takes different forms, which are divided between non-self-determination and self-determination:

- Avoiding a punishment or gaining a reward (external regulation). For example: it is the end of the day, the sun is shining, we are tempted to put off our task until tomorrow. However, we are motivated to finish the file to avoid hearing the piercing voice of our manager: "I told you this file was urgent! How am I meant to trust you if you never meet deadlines?" This is a non-self-determined form of motivation: we feel obliged to do it.
- Guilt (introjected regulation). For example: "If I do not finish this file today, Martina will have to make up for my delay and postpone her meeting with the director." This is a non-self-determined form of motivation: we force ourselves to do it.
- The possibility of reconciling the situation with other important activities or with meeting another objective (regulation through identification). For example: "Sometimes I have to work twice as hard to finish a task, but working part-time the following month allows me to take Lucy to her gymnastics classes, so come on, I can do it!" This is self-determined: we choose to do it, even if it is not wholly enjoyable.
- Sticking to my values and the principles that I have assumed (integrated regulation). For example: "I am someone who can be counted on, I have never left the office without finishing the file I was working on, whatever else I could be doing. It's a matter of principle! I will join you later." This is self-determined.

'Amotivation'

This refers to people who do their tasks with resignation, not noticing any relationship between their actions and the results, either for external reasons (no constructive feedback perceived), or for their own individual reasons (they still believe they are unable to meet objectives). This is the least self-determined form of motivation. It is not intentional, as the individual is acting neither out of choice nor for their own enjoyment.

Pelletier and Vallerand (cited in Laberon: 2011) observed that self-determined motivation (out of choice) has a significant impact on performance and positive effects at work. It would therefore allow us to better ensure performance and satisfaction than non-self-determined motivation (imposed).

In the table below, put a black cross next to your motivation at the time you started your job. Then put a red cross next to your current motivation.

		Statement	Motivation type
SELF-DETERMINED MOTIVATION	↑	"I do my work because it excites me, allows me to learn or helps me to feel fulfilled."	INTRINSIC MOTIVATION
		"My values are what guide my work; it is a matter of principal."	EXTRINSIC MOTIVATION: INTEGRATED REGULATION
		"I do my work because I can combine it with … and that is important to me, or because it allows me to reach another objective."	EXTRINSIC MOTIVATION: REGULATION THROUGH IDENTIFICATION
NON-SELF-DETERMINED MOTIVATION		"I do my work so that I do not feel guilty of…"	EXTRINSIC MOTIVATION: INTROJECTED REGULATION
		"I do my work to get … or to avoid …"	EXTRINSIC MOTIVATION: EXTERNAL REGULATION
	↓	"I am resigned and see no link between my actions and the results of my work."	AMOTIVATION

Regaining Motivation at Work © 50MINUTES.com

Have your motivations changed? On what level? What can you deduce from this? Is the currently dominant form of motivation compatible with the job you have? What should be changed? What can you change directly? What can you change indirectly? What can you not change?

WHY AM I UNMOTIVATED?

If we are motivated, it is, among other reasons, because we are interacting adequately with our professional context, and because we enjoy taking initiative over our behaviour (self-determination). If you have to regain your motivation, it is important to identify what might have impacted it. Many studies show that when the satisfaction of our needs for competency and self-determination are affected, our motivation decreases.

If you feel incompetent or you do not feel that you are at the origin of what you are doing, your intrinsic motivation (behaving out of choice or enjoyment) can decrease, as can some forms of extrinsic motivation (behaving to obtain or avoid something, or out of guilt). Studies indicate that if you feel like you are being kept under surveillance at work, if you are not receiving feedback or if your work is criticised, if your skills are called into question, or if you do not have enough room for manoeuvre to take initiatives, it would not be at all surprising if you felt unmotivated, were not performing as well and might want to quit your job.

SUFFER OR TAKE ACTION?

If the current situation is causing you to become unmotivated, do not wait for others to do something about it, change what you can! In his story *Who Moved My Cheese?*, the American psychologist and management consultant Spencer Johnson describes different ways of dealing with change.

Hem and Haw are looking for cheese, a condition of their wellbeing. While they have been used to always finding it in the same place, one day they are stunned: there is no more cheese! Not knowing 'who moved their cheese', each of the two companions develops his own strategy faced with this new situation:

- Hem passively waits for things to sort themselves out, preferring to be without cheese and tirelessly repeat the same fruitless behaviours rather than setting out into the maze with its unknown paths.
- Haw, despite also being tempted by this option initially, finally decides to stop kicking his heels. Accepting the idea that life is made up of a series of changes, and following his intuition, he sets off, with a knot in his stomach of fear of the unknown. Staying true to his mission, Haw gradually discovers a feeling of freedom. He ends up finding a "new cheese", which helps him, little by little, to forget what he had always known.

Do you feel unmotivated due to your current situation? What have you done to change it? How have you welcomed changes that have happened in your professional life? Do you simply want to wait for this to pass, like Hem? Or do you want to leave behind your fears and your old certainties to explore new opportunities and discover that you are also capable of appreciating new things, like Haw? How motivated are you to deal with change?

TOP TIPS

REVIEW YOUR CAREER

Where are you on your career path? What goals would you like to achieve?

GETTING 'RE-MOTIVATED': REFLECTION 4

The writer Yves Maire du Poset suggests mapping out your career on a graph. We have slightly adapted the exercise for you here.

- On the horizontal axis, write out the different stages of your career path.
- On the vertical axis, set out a satisfaction scale: 0 = not satisfied; +10 = very satisfied; -10 = very dissatisfied.

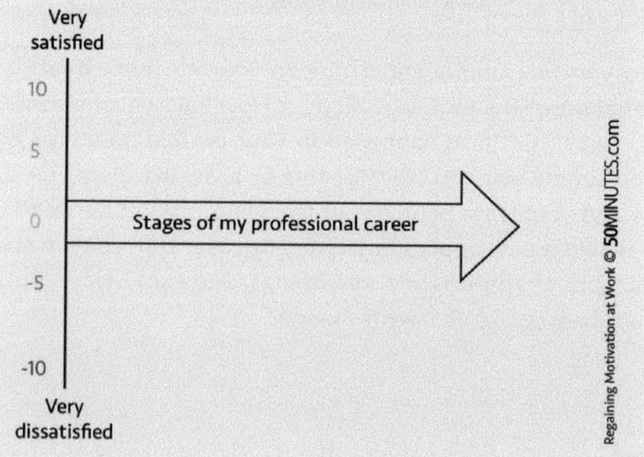

- For each key stage, indicate your level of satisfaction and join the dots together. Emphasise the best and most satisfying moments, as well as the moments in which your satisfaction was at its lowest.
- During those key moments, what was happening? Which factors influenced the situation? What were your expectations? To what extent were they met? What level of control did you have over the situation? Did you feel that you were able to act? Why?
- Next, take the time to describe two professional achievements that you were particularly proud of. Describe the situation, your objectives, the actions that you took and the results you obtained. What challenges were you facing? What were your factors of success? What do you want to do now? What do you need to do it?

REVIEW YOUR EMPLOYABILITY

According to the authors Müller and Djuatio, employability has different aspects:

- the ability to get a job (training)
- the ability to keep a job (mobility and development)
- the ability to find a new one (career management).

According to these authors, organisations have a lot to gain by improving the employability of their employees by increasing flexibility and mobility possibilities. On the one hand, this allows them to remain adaptable to changes in circumstances and, on the other hand, to promote the satisfaction of their staff and their commitment to the organisation. A positive perception of your employability improves your satisfaction at work.

GETTING 'RE-MOTIVATED': REFLECTION 5

Is my employability valued by my employer? (Questions inspired by Müller and Djuatio's research questionnaire, 2011).

Training

- Do you feel that your experience allows you to hold onto your job?
- Would your training allow you to be easily employed elsewhere in the general job market (training that offers mobility within or outside of the company)?
- Are you required to develop specific skills to keep your job?

Mobility within the organisation

- Have you had continual training, or do you have the opportunity to receive it in the future?
- Does this training allow you to adapt to changes in your company?
- Does this training allow you to respond to changes in technology within your company?

REVIEW YOUR EMOTIONAL COMMITMENT TO THE ORGANISATION

Commitment to an organisation is representative of agreement with its aims and values, a desire to make an effort for its benefit and a wish to remain a member. We can distinguish:

- Continuation commitment, which is your instrumental link to the organisation, in which leaving it is more costly than remaining in it;
- Normative commitment, which forces people to stay out of moral obligation;
- Emotional commitment, which refers to your emotional link with the organisation.

The latter is influenced by:

- the nature of our work (variety of tasks, degree of independence, positive feedback, etc.)
- interactions between the working group and the boss (commitment increases when our boss includes us in decisions)
- company culture
- the role that we play within the organisation.

DID YOU KNOW?

Psychology identifies three different types of work-related problems that can cause stress and therefore have an impact on our health:

- the job's ambiguity, when we don't know exactly what is expected of us;
- role conflict, when the tasks we receive are in contradiction with contextual elements;
- overwork, when we have too much work for the role that we have been assigned.

These situations, which affect our health, have negative consequences on motivation at work. How do you feel in the role that you have been given at the moment?

REVIEW YOUR NEEDS FOR RESPECT AND RECOGNITION

In their work *Searching for the Human in Human Resource Management* (2007), Bolton and Houlihan illustrate that we either suffer or feel fulfilled depending on the extent to which our needs are being met. Human beings are not content with feeling secure, enjoying good material conditions or having access to opportunities; we also need recognition, respectful and non-embarrassing interactions with others and external approval. We need to feel integrated and to feel that we are supported by a network.

The weight of the rules of your company has an impact on your behaviour and that of the people around you at work. Beyond the stated rules and procedures, there is a web of less obvious conventions that will influence your wellbeing at work. The professional contexts in which we evolve value different virtues or vices, and encourage some behaviours more than others. Researchers have shown that we do not really work to boost our self-esteem, but rather because most of us think it is the right thing to do, and that it will earn us the approval of those around us.

If you feel competent, you like your job and your colleagues are pleasant, but you are still suffering from demotivation, take the time to analyse the valued criteria in your professional context. To what extent do you agree with them? To what extent do you disagree? To what extent do you feel valued and respected? What would you need for this to be the case? What kind of professional context would be able to meet your needs?

REVIEW YOUR SENSE OF FAIRNESS

Feelings of respect and self-esteem are also related to fee-lings of fairness. Perhaps you feel demotivated because one of your colleagues got a promotion but you felt that they didn't really deserve it? Feelings of unfairness at work, parti-cularly those linked to differences in salary, valuing of skills and treatment in working conditions, affect motivation. Several studies have illustrated the influence of fairness on satisfaction. It can be distributive (linked to personal motivation, fairness perceived in terms of the distribution of resources, such as salary, satisfaction related to what we earn and to our work) or procedural (fairness linked to the methods used by the organisation, to the structure of the organisation and to our commitment to the company).

<u>**GETTING 'RE-MOTIVATED': REFLECTION 6**</u>

Do you feel this is fair?
(Questions inspired by Müller and Djuatio's research questionnaire, 2011).

Distribution of resources

- Do you feel that your company offers you more advantages than a competitor could offer you?
- Do you feel that your salary matches the position you are in?
- Does your salary match your level of skill?

- Does your salary match your level of responsibi-
  lity?
- If you compare your advantages and contributions
  to those of people who are in similar positions,
  does the situation seem fair to you?

Methods and procedures used by your organisation

- Do you feel you are able to give your opinion?
- Can you easily give your opinion on some of the
  company's decisions?
- Does your company communicate simply about its
  decisions?
- Does the company deal with your training requests
  quickly?
- Do you feel that the company takes your opinion
  into consideration when making decisions?
- Do you feel a sense of unfairness? Do you feel that
  what you get matches what you expect? What can
  you do to improve the situation? How might you
  formulate constructive requests, and to whom
  would you be inclined to address them to improve
  your sense of fairness and regain your motivation?

LOOK OBJECTIVELY AT THE IMPACT OF THE HARMFUL THINGS THAT SABOTAGE YOUR MOTIVATION

In his work *The No Asshole Rule*, Robert Sutton, a management professor at the Stanford Engineering School,
suggests an approach which turns the interpretation on

its head and imagines reversing the trend when faced with being undermined by a person who uses all their energy to make our lives difficult or lower our morale. These "assholes" harm our performance and consequently that of the whole company.

If your motivation is being impacted by one of these "assholes", you have probably observed behaviour such as: invasion of personal space, threats and intimidation, sarcastic jokes, public humiliation, among others. According to the author, all companies should adopt the "no asshole rule", in order to conserve the energy and self-esteem of their victims, as well as their performance.

But how do we deal with an "asshole"? Simply by objectively noting the hours you have lost by being in contact with them and representing them as costs. If you take a few moments to calculate the time wasted with hierarchy, human resources, external parties, recruitment following departures or absences, additional hours, exchanges of emails, meetings, phone interviews, etc., you will be able to calculate the cost that the useless interactions with this person incur. If your emotional arguments are not heard, the cost that can be attributed to damages and the amount of time you have wasted will act as an objective basis for discussion. And while you are calculating the financial impact of their toxicity, keep your distance from these individuals as much as you can!

GET WHAT YOU WANT BY SHARING WHAT MOTIVATES YOU

Perhaps you feel unmotivated because you feel that some of your colleagues are bold enough to present themselves in a better light and end up getting exactly what you want? Pelletier and Vallerand draw our attention to the fact that when performance is equal, people who show intrinsic motivation (a desire to exceed their own expectations, to develop, to be fulfilled) are generally perceived as more 'socially desirable', while people with defined (not imposed) but extrinsic motivation (for example the aim of reconciling their personal and professional lives) are perceived as more 'useful', because they are more efficient.

The kind of motivation that we demonstrate may therefore have an impact on our interviewers! The perverse nature of this process invites candidates to present intrinsic motivations solely to come across well, which does not always gain the sympathy of others. Be aware that your employer may appreciate different kinds of motivation depending on what expectations they have of you.

FAQS

TO REGAIN MOTIVATION AT WORK, SHOULD I FOCUS SOLELY ON PROFESSIONAL ASPECTS?

No – the lack of motivation you are feeling at work is probably the result of broader wellbeing problems, which cover all aspects of your life. Your attempts at getting 're-motivated' should therefore be part of an overall reflection on this.

If you work solely on the aspects that affect you at work, you will certainly notice an improvement; but to deal with difficult situations, it is not enough to reduce your contact with sources of displeasure. This attitude will help you to protect yourself, but it will not necessarily make you happier. It is therefore just as important for you to be aware of what is happening in your life outside of work.

Studies have shown that, after a traumatic event or a culmination of tension, the most common cause of depression is a lack of enjoyable events and activities in our lives. Researchers, including behaviourists (members of a psychological school centred on changing behaviour), starting from the observation that happiness is not simply the opposite of unhappiness, agree on the fact that increasing these activities has a positive effect on our mood. Thus, as well as removing sources of suffering, we need to develop behaviour that brings us pleasure and joy.

If you are feeling unmotivated, it is perhaps time to think about how many enjoyable things you have done recently. Does your life contain enjoyable activities that give you energy and help you to revitalise yourself? Have you taken a holiday recently?

My company tells me to be proactive, but values those who don't rock the boat...

You are giving it your best shot, trying to offer innovative solutions and show that you are proactive. You are convinced that this is what your company expects from you, because that is what is written in your job description. However, your motivation is being affected by stone-faced colleagues who never take risks and yet, for reasons unknown to you, always end up as the favourites!

The concept of adhering to the norms of loyalty explains that the person who avoids any behaviour that could be socially called into question, and who does not spend their time challenging the hierarchy or the power of the system, thus embodying the loyal and faithful co-worker, will be more appreciated. Why? Their behaviour maintains the balance of the social environment and keeps authority in its place.

It is not necessarily your skills that should be called into question! The best way of counterbalancing this effect is to show your added value – do not simply wait for someone to notice it – and make your mark.

HOW SHOULD I COPE WITH PROFESSIONAL STRESS THAT REDUCES MY MOTIVATION?

Scientific literature tells us that there are three 'coping methods' (Rillaer: 1992) that help us to resist stress effectively:

- Thinking that we are able to act in a way that influences what is happening around us (collecting information, analysing, taking initiatives);
- Welcoming change positively by perceiving it as an opportunity that is part of life;
- Seeing work as something that is interesting rather than alienating.

The people who combine these three methods will be bolder and more energetic than others, as their 'solution-focused' approach to developing new behaviour will allow them to adjust to the events that arise in their setting.

HOW CAN I COME UP WITH SOLUTIONS WHEN FACED WITH DIFFICULT SITUATIONS?

Here are a few steps to follow to come up with solutions when faced with a problematic and demotivating situation.

- To start with, stop and look at the problem in front of you.
- Formulate it by studying the situation and describing what you would like to change.
- Look for solutions, but do not simply accept those that are easily accessible. Instead, imagine new solutions by

applying the following principles:

- Do not believe the evidence and consider your interpretation of the problem as one of many;
- Have a detached view of the situation, by trying to identify the relationship between the different aspects of the problem and the heart of the problem itself;
- Break the problem up into sub-problems and order them;
- Refer to solutions that have been used in the past;
- Seek advice from people who have already been in identical situations;
- Get informed using experts;
- Imagine what you would say to another person in your situation;
- Consider these ideas without rejecting them outright.

- Choose the appropriate solution, by evaluating its feasibility and reflecting on the short-term costs and benefits, but also on those over the medium and long term.

- Implement your decisions by setting deadlines, visualising positive consequences, treating the solution as an experience, setting yourself reasonable objectives, beginning with actions that bring you satisfaction and a sense of achievement to get started, and above all by taking action instead of just discussing the problem.

- Evaluate the effects of these solutions to keep up your motivation.

WOULD I BE MORE SATISFIED AND MOTIVATED IF I WORKED PART TIME?

Not necessarily. Studies carried out in France indicate that part-time employees are satisfied overall. However, this satisfaction is counterbalanced by dissatisfaction regarding their ability to take part in decision-making, to the recognition of the work they have done and to stress experienced at work (as the reduced working hours are not always proportional to the reduced workload, these employees are paid less and have no chance of being promoted, etc.). The people who do not necessarily envisage 'career progression' are generally more satisfied with this option than those who are aiming for professional development or see this solution as a transition period during a career change.

HOW DO PEOPLE ADAPT TO ORGANISATIONAL CHANGES?

Many organisations deal with change, and adapt their structure and procedures to the search for efficiency. These changes can constitute a threat to job security, impacting our working relationships and our private life, and affecting our wellbeing, professional status, self-confidence and identity. There are many things that can make our situations uncomfortable and generate anxiety. Terry and Callan have addressed the question of adjusting, by studying factors that allow us to predict the thoughts and actions that will be developed to solve problems when faced with stress in the context of change. This is what they discovered:

- We need to consider the characteristics of change, as its implications are not identical for everyone. We need to take into account its effects on work, the extent to which we believe we can be involved in its implementation (the participatory approach often being the key to success in organisational change), our feelings of control over the event, notably driven by the clarity (or lack thereof) of the leader's vision.

- Our interpretation of change will also be influential. Thus, people who feel that they can act on factors of stress to reduce them and who feel able to adopt the necessary behaviour to prove themselves in a given situation will tend to keep up their efforts to manage it. On the other hand, the people who doubt their ability to respond to the demands of the organisation following this change risk concentrating on a feeling of incompetence that will make it difficult for them to handle the situation.

- The people who implement coping strategies (allowing them to deal with stress), thoughts and behaviour in view of finding solutions, are more likely to adapt to change and to deal with professional stress. On the other hand, 'emotion-focused' people, who do not concentrate on the problem but remain overwhelmed by their level of emotional distress linked to the change, will not adapt as well.

- Internal resources will also influence a person's reactions to a situation: personal characteristics, self-confidence, the feeling of having control over their fate, their social resources and their perceived sources of support at work – which, moreover, will have a greater effect than resources outside of the world of work.

If you are feeling unmotivated because you feel threatened by change, we recommend getting informed and evaluating the extent to which you can get involved rather than avoiding the unpleasant sensations caused by the situation. If you adopt a 'solution-focused' attitude, this should increase your feelings of control and reduce the feeling of being threatened and consequently stressed.

SHOULD I THINK ABOUT CHANGING CAREER PATH TO REGAIN MY MOTIVATION?

Potentially, but not without preparation or without taking some risks. Have you figured out what is causing your lack of motivation at work? Have you tried to look at the situation objectively and implemented solutions, and yet doubt and dissatisfaction persist? Then it's true that it might be time to think about changing direction. The support of those around you will be very important in this process. The time has come to establish a new plan. Catherine Négroni, in her book about voluntary professional reorientation, sets out different kinds of reorientation:

- Passion-based reorientation, to live a hobby and discover a passion;
- Promotional reorientation, for learning or making up for a feeling of academic failure;
- Job stability reorientation, for gaining stability, finding a sense of belonging and anticipating the future;
- Balance reorientation, to slow down by finding a balance between professional and private life.

What type of reorientation would you like to undertake? What would your dream be? If you anchor this dream in reality, what does your objective become? What is your situation in terms of skills, training, resources, etc.? What are the intermediate stages for meeting your objective? What do you need? Who can help you? What aspects of your professional past can you use as a resource for building your future? Professional reorientation is a project that is successfully carried out by engaging in self-reflection and interacting with others: it is facilitated by their support.

OVER TO YOU

It is time to get your motivation back, first of all by analysing what might be affecting it. Briefly comment on each of the following points.

Point of analysis	Comment
The respect of your values or particular ethics	
Your independence	
The support you feel you receive from your colleagues, manager and organisation	
The usefulness of your work	
Opportunities to learn	
Recognition from members of your organisation, clients, etc.	
The quality of your relationships at work	
The pleasure you derive from doing your work	
Your role within the organisation	
The extent to which you fit in with company culture	
Other	

Secondly, look for solutions by structuring your reflection using the IDEAL model.

	Method	Your response
I	**Identify problems** – identify the cause of your lack of motivation.	
D	**Define and represent the problems** – describe the events that in your opinion triggered your loss of motivation, what you noticed, thought, dealt with, etc. Try to describe the events objectively. Note the emotions that you felt (fear, anger, sadness, etc.). Express your needs when dealing with these events.	
E	**Explore possible strategies** – explore the alternatives, the possibilities for exchanging, delegating, removing certain activities. Could the availability of methods, tools and training help you? What kind of help do you need? What are your ideas and suggestions?	
A	**Act on strategies** – what practical actions could you take? How? With whom? How long would it take? What would be the benefits and costs? Establish a plan of action and discuss it with your manager (or, in case of a disagreement, with an HR representative or member of support staff appointed in the context of the law on wellbeing at work).	
L	**Look back and evaluate the effects of your activities** – agree on a deadline for implementing the plan of action and a moment for evaluating its effects in order to move onto the likely necessary adjustments.	

(Source: Bransford and Stein, 1984: 12).

We want to hear from you!
Leave a comment on your online library
and share your favourite books on social media!

FURTHER READING

BIBLIOGRAPHY

- Bolton, S. and Houlihan, M. (2007) *Searching for the Human in Human Resource Management. Theory, Practice and Workplace Contexts.* New York: Palgrave Macmillan.
- Bransford, J. and Stein, B. (1984) *The Ideal Problem Solver: Guide for Improving Thinking and Creativity.* Wallingford: W. H. Freeman and Company.
- Cobut, E. and Bomal, G. (2009) *Motiver, être motivé et réussir ensemble.* Liège: Edipro.
- Gangloff, B. (2011) La norme d'allégeance. *Psychologie et recrutement. Modèles, pratiques et normativités.* Brussels: De Boeck, pp. 177-197.
- Johnson, S. (1999) *Who Moved My Cheese: An Amazing Way to Deal with Change in Your Work and in Your Life.* London: Vermilion.
- Le Saget, M. (1992) *Le management intuitif. Une nouvelle force.* Paris: Dunod.
- Maire Du Poset, Y. (2013) *Décrochez le job de vos rêves. Un guide incontournable pour obtenir le poste que vous voulez.* Paris: Leduc Éditions.
- Meyer, J. (1997) Organizational Commitment. *International Review of Industrial and Organizational Psychology*, 12. Chichester: John Wiley and Sons, pp. 175-228.
- Morin, E. (2003) Sens du travail, définition, mesure et validation. *Dimensions individuelles et sociales de l'investissement professionnel*, 2. Louvain-La-Neuve: Presses universitaires de Louvain, pp. 11-20.

- Müller, J. and Djuatio, E. (2011) Les relations entre la justice organisationnelle, l'employabilité, la satisfaction et l'engagement organisationnel des salariés. *Revue de gestion des ressources humaines*. [Online]. Vol. 82(4), pp. 46-62. [Accessed 18 November 2016]. Available from: <http://www.cairn.info/article.php?ID_ARTICLE=GRHU_082_0046&DocId=74336&hits=11206+11197+11195+11194+6499+6494+6492+6491+14+6+5+3+2+>
- Négroni, C. (2007) *Reconversion professionnelle volontaire. Changer d'emploi, changer de vie. Un regard sociologique sur les bifurcations*. Paris: Armand Colin.
- Rosa, C. (2003) Développement de carrière et intersignifications des milieux de vie des salariés à temps partiel. *Dimensions individuelles et sociales de l'investissement professionnel*, 2. Louvain-La-Neuve: Presses universitaires de Louvain, pp. 49-58.
- Sutton, R. (2007) *The No Asshole Rule: Building a Civilised Workplace and Surviving One That Isn't*. London: Sphere.
- Terry, D. and Callan, V. (2000) Employee adjustment to an organizational change: a stress and coping perspective. *Coping, health and organizations. Issues in occupational health*. London: Taylor and Francis, pp. 259-275.
- Van Rillaer, J. (1992) *La gestion de soi*. Liège: Mardaga.

ADDITIONAL SOURCES

- Achor, S. (2010) *The Happiness Advantage: The Seven Principles of Positive Psychology that Fuel Success and Performance at Work*. London: Ebury.

- Amor, M. and Pellew, A. (2016) *The Idea in You: How to Find It, Build It, and Change Your Life*. New York: Portfolio Penguin.
- Klein, H., Becker, T. and Meyer, J. (2009) *Commitment in organizations*. London: Routledge.

50MINUTES.com

IMPROVE YOUR GENERAL KNOWLEDGE

IN A BLINK OF AN EYE !

www.50minutes.com

www.50minutes.com

Ebook EAN: 9782806289100

Paperback EAN: 9782806289117

Legal Deposit: D/2016/12603/738

Cover: © Primento

Digital conception by Primento, the digital partner of publishers.